AF245585

When
school bells
rang

the history of the Wilmot, New Hampshire schools

When school bells rang

Florence Langley

PHOENIX PUBLISHING
Canaan, New Hampshire

Langley, Florence, 1902-
   When school bells rang.

   Includes index.
   1. Education — New Hampshire — Wilmot — History. 2. Wilmot, N.H. — Schools — History. I. Title.
   LA330.W54L36   371'.009742'72   76-50006
   ISBN 0-914016-34-2

Printed in the United States of America
by Courier Printing Company

Binding by New Hampshire Bindery

Design by A.L. Morris

CONTENTS

PREFACE

THE HISTORY OF A TOWN would be incomplete without the story of its schools. From the time of its incorporation until June 30, 1967, Wilmot maintained schools within its borders. After this date the town became a part of the Kearsarge Regional School District, represented by a school board member. Grades one through eight attend school in New London while grades nine through twelve are sent to Kearsarge Regional High School in Sutton.

To write the history of the early schools is like trying to put a jigsaw puzzle together. Separate facts gleaned from reports of town clerk and treasurer, school reports in the annual town report, the clerks' reports of the various school districts previous to 1886 (very few of which could be found), make up the various pieces of the puzzle. These I have tried to fit together along with recollections of elderly citizens. Readers should allow for a margin of error and for some lost pieces of the puzzle.

Dates become tiresome but are necessary in a history. It is recognized that part of the material will be of little interest to some people. As I tried to sort out the what, when, how and why of events, I frequently wished some of my questions had recorded answers. It is with this in mind that I beg indulgence if too much material seems to have been written. Frequently I have quoted from reports, for the words and language of such add interest. Names of people help to point out where they resided in town. I regret that I did not pay more attention to what my parents and others related of school history and other happenings dealing with the town and its citizens. It is with this in mind that I have written this book before past history can be lost.

F.L. / July 4, 1976

When school bells rang

School Administration

Financial Support of Schools

A T THE FIRST TOWN MEETING in 1808 it was voted to raise two hundred dollars for schooling. In November that year a vote was taken to see if the town would take a part of this money to help defray town charges, but the vote was against doing this. By a vote in 1813 the sum necessary to defray town charges was taken from the interest money and the rest was used for schooling.

The schools were chiefly supported by the town. Of the taxes paid under five different headings in 1820 one was a school tax and another a schoolhouse tax. The latter was for building and repairing schoolhouses, and it was raised by the town and assessed to the property owners in each school district. By law the state required each town to raise a certain amount on each dollar of the proportion for public taxes. In 1808 the assessment was seventy dollars on each dollar of valuation, ten years later this sum was raised to ninety dollars. The amount was raised from time to time until in 1870 it was three hundred and fifty dollars.

Another source of town revenue for the schools was the dog tax. In 1887 this was sixty-five dollars. This tax continued to be used for school purposes until 1936.

The first financial aid came from the state under the title of the Literary Fund. This fund was created by an act of the legislature in 1828; it was distributed to each town in November. All banks in the state were taxed at the rate of one-half of one percent on their capital stock, the money to be used for the support of public schools. The amount each town received was in proportion to the number of scholars, not less than five years of age, who from reports of school superintendents attended the public schools not less than two weeks within that year. Wilmot received $68.62 in 1852. At that time there were thirteen school districts. The money was to be used as other school money. After 1919 this fund was no longer available.

It may be of interest to compare the amount received for public education with that spent for town and county paupers and for highways. For the year ending March 1, 1880, it was recorded that $561.18 was paid out for town paupers, $629.25 for county paupers, and $306.32 for highway bills. School tax as raised by law was $623; school money voted by the town, $150, with $58.46 received from the Literary Fund. At this time there was an enrollment of two hundred pupils in the fall term from eleven of the thirteen schools. Figures on pupil enrollment for Districts Nos. 2 and 11 were not available as the teachers failed to pass in their registers.

By the law of 1885 the assessed valuation of the school building in each district was rebated to the several taxpayers their pro rata proportion of the value of the schoolhouse belonging to each respectively. Total for the town was $1,393.63.

State regulations regarding schools continued and, of course, resulted in increased tax budgets. In 1919 medical inspection was made mandatory, transportation for all pupils below the ninth grade who lived more than two miles from a school was required, and a superintendent had to be employed (by this time Wilmot already had a superintendent). State aid for supervision was now out and in its place there was a two dollar a head tax for all pupils registered. These were a few of the changes in the overall picture.

For the school year ending June 30, 1965, only the schools at the Center and at the Flat kept; the whole number of pupils registered in grades one through eight was sixty-three. Total net expenditures for the year were $24,904.83, of this $6,776.19 was for secondary tuitions. Receipts from local taxation were $23,711.06, from sweepstakes $1,601.62; making the grand total net receipts $25,312.68.

Superintending School Committee

The law of 1827 required that each town at its annual meeting in March elect by ballot a Superintending School Committee consisting of not less than three, nor more than five, persons. Later in 1867 the law was changed to read "a school committee of so many persons as they think fit, and whenever any town shall neglect to choose such committee the selectmen before the 20th of April shall appoint such committee." Previous to this year and under the date of March 10, 1847, we read "Otis Jones was appointed Superintending School Committee by the selectmen as there was a vacancy, also John Brown and Merrill Cross." Again in April, 1848, and 1851 three men were appointed to fill vacancies. Did the citizens fail to elect the committee at its March meeting, did the elected officials resign, or did they move to another town?*

It was also the duty of this committee to examine the teachers who made application, to visit and inspect every school at least twice a year, and to examine the proficiency of the scholars. In return for all this he (probably the chairman) would receive a "reasonable compensation" from the town. William Flanders received ten dollars in 1852, whereas in 1878 the Superintending School Committee was paid fifty dollars.

The printed report of the committee varied greatly. Some went into great detail relative to each teacher, her personality and performance. Such evaluations were very frank. One can picture the disagreements and arguments which probably resulted. This is evidenced by the town meeting in 1845 when the selectmen were instructed to appoint the committee with orders from the voters *not* to visit the schools. Fred E. Goodhue, as the Superintending School Committee in 1884-1885, realized the limitations of these school visits for he wrote in his report, "It is exceedingly difficult to arrive at just conclusions as to the success of a school by simply spending a few hours in it."

A common thread of criticism ran through many of the reports.

---

*The Superintending School Committee was to present an annual report to the town giving the number of weeks the schools had been kept in each district for each term, what proportion had been kept by male and what portion by female teachers, the number of scholars who attended each school, progress made in each school in the various branches of learning, and the number of children between the ages of four and fourteen in each district who had not attended school. This report was included in the same publication as the town report. Apparently only the name of the chairman was signed to this.

Parents were taken to task for their disinterestedness in the schools. It was felt that they should visit the schools more often. Advice to parents in 1885 is as good today as it was then:

Opinions respecting schools should not be based upon rumor, nor upon reports brought by the children. The pupil whose misconduct has made him the subject of correction has seldom a good word for his instructor. With the best intentions, children have not sufficient maturity of mind, and are not as pupils in a position to interpret correctly the feelings or judge the conduct of the teacher. Parents should therefore suspend judgment upon incidents of the school until consultation with the teacher, who in most cases, will be able to make satisfactory explanations.

It can be seen that the Superintending School Committee was a responsible position in the early history of Wilmot Schools.

Prudential Committee

Back in 1800 the state government set up the "Prudential Committee" plan. Each school district was an entity as far as control of the school within its borders was concerned. This committee usually consisted of one or more members, but the law directed that it should not exceed three.

The annual meeting of each school district was required by law to be held in the month of March. Warning of the meeting was to be posted by the Prudential Committee on the door of the schoolhouse at least seven days prior to the meeting and before March 15th. If there were no schoolhouse in the district, and this was true in at least one case, the Prudential Committee must give notice to each legal voter in the district or leave such notice at his dwelling place. To make it legal he must appear before the justice of the peace and swear that this had been done. Thus, an item in the clerk's book for District No. 1 reads:

This certifies that I posted up a true copy of the Warrant attested on the door of the schoolhouse in Said District on the seventh day of March, 1869 and on the same day I posted up a like copy at the Store of Prescott and Woodward, being one of the most public places in Said District—A.B. Putnam, Prudential Committee.

Sometimes the Prudential Committee was remiss in posting the warrant. The law had provided for such a contingency. Three or more voters of the district could then make written application to the Prudential Committee for a special meeting. If this application was neglected for ten days then three or more voters could apply to the selectmen whose duty it was to post a warrant calling for such a meeting.

In 1856 three voters in the White District appealed to the selectmen to appoint "some suitable person to be the Prudential Committee as a vacancy now exists by reason of not being qualified as the law directs." Evidence would seem to indicate that this particular committee was not a legal voter in that district. The law stated that if he was "incompetent, or irresponsible or mismanaged the affairs of the district" he could be dismissed on petition of one-fourth of the legal voters of the district.

Seventeen years later the Superintending School Committee in its report to the state wrote, "The office of Prudential Committee should be abolished. Like the President they have too many friends and relatives."

Sometimes it was difficult to secure anyone to serve on the committee. We can understand the reluctance of an individual to accept this office when the law read,

It shall be the duty of the Prudential Committee to select and hire teachers for the district, provide for their board, furnish necessary fuel, make such occasional repairs in the school house and furniture as may be necessary, not exceeding in amount five per cent of the school money for the district, notify the Superintending School Committee of the commencement of the summer and winter school and give them all such information and assistance as may be necessary for the performance of their duties.

Fortunately, many of these duties were taken care of by the voters in their annual district meeting.

School Boards and School Meetings

In 1886 the legislature passed a law whereby each town would elect a school board having direct control of all school matters. How this was received by the citizens is recorded in the 1886-87 report of the first school board: "At the commencement of the school year there was much feeling against the adoption of the town system of schools.

This feeling was carried to such an extent that the educational interests of the town were sadly neglected. By this we mean the refusal of the citizens to provide suitable money for school purposes." Members of the board were Julius B. Hale, John M. Carr, and Minot Stearns. There were still thirteen schools at this time, and the amount of money raised was $581 (the amount required by law). One hundred and thirty-nine dollars and sixty-nine cents were received from the Literary Fund and $22.00 from the dog tax, a total of $742.69. The previous year the whole amount of school money paid out was $1,069.76.

The warrant for the annual school meeting was first published in the town report in 1904. This particular warrant carried eight articles. A moderator, clerk, treasurer, and a member of the school board were to be elected. The meeting was held in the schoolhouse at the Center. For a while the meeting was held the afternoon of town meeting day. As the amount of town business transacted increased the school meeting was changed to a different day.

The first woman to serve on the board was Harriet K. Whittemore. Between the years of 1933 and 1952 the entire three-member school board consisted of women. During another period Ernest Howard served a total of seventeen years. It was not always easy to find someone to serve on the board, and one year ballots were cast seven times before this was accomplished.

The clerk recorded a few interesting bits of business. For instance, in 1926 a motion was made and carried that the town not raise two hundred dollars for the superintendent's excess salary. Then a motion was before the house to raise one hundred dollars for this purpose. This motion was amended to read "that $199.99 be raised for the Superintendent's excess salary," and the vote was in the affirmative.

Apparently the State Board of Health issued a directive in regard to improvement of school toilets, for in the clerk's record for 1917 we read that the following motion was made and carried: "I move that we fail to act on the writ of the Board of Health in the matter of repairs, and we will stand out and fight. We also appropriate the sum of fifty dollars for legal expense of the School Board." At a special meeting in May the report of the counsel was given: "We have looked the matter over and have come to the conclusion that the repairs required by Dr. Watson could be enforced against the district. The statute seems to be broad enough to cover everything which he had recommended to be done." It is, therefore, not surprising to find that the following year

                    When School Bells Rang

$353.67 was expended for construction of new toilets. Apparently this was at the Center and at the Flat.

An important business of the school meeting was to raise and appropriate money for the support of schools. In 1893 there were three attempts to do this. One vote was *not* to raise any money for school purposes. Finally the vote was to raise one mill per dollar of valuation for repair of schoolhouses. It was at the school meeting that the voters also decided on sale of old schoolhouses, major repairs on the buildings, and the re-opening of a schoolhouse.

The last school meeting of the town of Wilmot was held March 11, 1967. Officers elected were to serve only until July first of that year as on that date Wilmot became a member of the Kearsarge Regional School District. This decision had been reached at a special meeting February 19, 1959, when it was voted to petition the State Board of Education to become a member of a regional school district which would include a group of neighboring towns. The vote was thirty-five in favor and thirteen opposed. Final approval on May 2, 1966, resulted in New London, Springfield, Bradford, Newbury, Sutton, Warner, and Wilmot becoming members of the Kearsarge Regional School District.

State Supervision of Education

In the early years there was little state supervision of education. We do know that in 1864 there were "County Commissioners of Common Schools." Apparently it was their duty to visit at least one school in each town. These reports were printed, and that for 1864 was the eighteenth annual report. Silvanus Hayward was commissioner for Merrimack County and this is what he wrote for that year:

Tuesday morning, December 15, 1863, the roads were dangerous with ice, I however made my way from Andover to Wilmot. At Wilmot visited only one school. The house was new but evidently built with an eye to economy rather than convenience. The school did not impress me favorably. Ten classes in arithmetic and other like arrangements so cut up the day that but little could be well done. The house in which I was to speak was already occupied for a temperance lecture by Mr. Fitzgerald, he however commenced early and I addressed about sixty people the last of the evening.

In 1897 groups of towns were authorized by the state to join together in supervisory unions with each union to hire a superintendent among them. The state would pay one-half of the superintendent's salary. In 1915 the town of Wilmot voted to employ such a superintendent and became a part of Supervisory Union No. 1. Idella K. Farnum was the first superintendent, and she served in this capacity until 1925. The unions were changed from time to time, and by 1958 Wilmot was a part of Supervisory Union No. 46.

Wilmot had twenty-five weeks of school in 1905, and thirty in 1917. Previously the figure varied with the individual schools. By 1919 schools were required to be in session for 36 weeks or 180 days which is true today.

Teachers were required to keep a careful check of attendance in the school register. The towns were supposed to appoint a truant officer, but in some cases the school board served as such. In addition the truant officer, or other agent of the school board was required to take a census every September of all children in the district between five and sixteen years of age.

The School Attendance Law stated that all children must attend a public or an approved private school every day that school was in session from their eighth to sixteenth birthdays, or to their fourteenth birthday if they had completed the 8th grade. Later the law was changed so that children from six to sixteen years must attend school. Younger children could attend at the discretion of the local school board. A few children five years of age were in some of the Wilmot schools in 1914, but in 1938 the board made the following ruling: "No pupil will be allowed to enter the first grade unless he will be six years of age on the first of January following the opening of school in September." At one time, probably around 1919, a school transportation law directed the district to furnish transportation to all pupils below the 9th grade who lived more than two miles from the school to which they were assigned.

Various laws relating to education were passed from time to time, but without doubt the most important one was that of 1919 creating a State Board of Education. It consisted of five members appointed by the governor with the governor as an ex officio member. Tenure of office was five years.

The board was given the power of management, supervision, and direction of all public schools and was authorized to appoint a Commissioner of Education and four deputy commissioners. Twelve important powers and duties were given to the board. Among the

When School Bells Rang

most important were authority to combine the several school districts in the state into supervisory unions and establish the superintendents' salaries, supervision of the expenditures of state appropriations for education, recommending to the legislature needed changes in existing laws, and preparation and publication of diagrams and outlines of courses for the schools. It can be seen that the State Board of Education has been, and continues to be, a power in the educational system of New Hampshire.

At this time the state began to take a more active part in education. Two facts were evident: the belief that teachers needed to be better qualified, and that children should be in school and in good health if they were to benefit from the education offered. In order to teach one needed to have a temporary certificate, a state certificate, a license or a permit. Around 1915 graduates of the teachers' course of one year at one of the two state normal schools were granted certificates attesting to this training. They could, in some cases, secure a state certificate by passing additional examinations or by filing proof of additional education. A regular course of two years at either of the normal schools entitled one to a permanent elementary state teacher's certificate. An item in the Wilmot School Report for the year ending June 30, 1934, stated that of its four teachers three had state certificates and one a license. In some instances a girl graduating from high school wished to teach that fall. Such a person was required to take a summer course of six weeks. This was the start of a teaching career for several individuals. To encourage attendance at a state normal school tuition was free to any New Hampshire resident who agreed to teach in the state the number of years he had attended such a school.

Another way of attracting better qualified teachers for one-room schools was to require attendance at two yearly county institutes. They were conducted under the direction of the State Board of Education and were mainly concerned with the immediate needs of rural teachers. Since attendance was required, these one-day institutes could count as school days.

State aid to a school district resulted indirectly in more qualified teachers since a town was enabled to pay higher salaries and thus attract the better teachers. Naturally the town had to meet certain requirements in order to receive this aid. If the tax of five dollars on a thousand dollars of the value of the ratable estates in the district was insufficient, the state board provided the balance of the money necessary to maintain the required elementary schools. Wilmot benefitted from this arrangement.

Two acts, the Medical Inspection Act and the Child Health Recovery Act, had a direct influence on the health of school children, and also on the school budget. The State Board of Education made the regulation that all districts which had not adopted medical inspection had to employ a school physician or school nurse for the physical examination of children. As far back as 1927 Wilmot voted to adopt medical inspection and to hire a physician. However, in 1934 the town voted to repeal this action and to employ a school nurse instead. The annual report of the school nurse was a part of the school report, and thereby parents were made aware of her work and the health of the school children as a whole. In 1930 about one dollar and a half per pupil was allowed for medical supervision in state-aided districts when a full-time school nurse was employed.

Teachers

While the district system was in effect the teachers were selected and hired by the various prudential committees. Sometimes at their annual meeting the voters of a district would express their preference as to the sex of the teacher. A mistress was more apt to teach the summer school. Male teachers were more difficult to secure, and when their names did appear, they were usually found as teachers for the winter session. District No. 1 went so far one year as to vote that, "H.B. Dow have the opportunity to teach school in said district if he will accept."

More boys and older boys were likely to attend school in the winter since they were less needed for work on the farm, and therefore it was felt that a male teacher was desirable. Some of the boys would be well up in their teens. For instance, in a school in the northern part of the town in 1848-1849 the oldest boy was twenty, one was sixteen, one boy seventeen, and another boy (or should we say young man) was nineteen. This school opened December 25 and closed February 27. It was taught by Elisha K. Morrill. There were nineteen boys and four girls enrolled. Six of the boys were sons of "Blacksmith" Langley and three, the sons of Samuel Langley.

As has been previously noted the state required the Superintending School Committee to report annually what portion of school had been kept by male and what portion by female teachers. In the

When School Bells Rang

school year 1879-1880 eighteen teachers were employed, three were male and fifteen were female. Ten of these were residents of Wilmot. Five of the eighteen had never taught. There were thirteen school districts at this time.

The state law required that the school master or school mistress should be a citizen of the United States, of good moral character, and well qualified to teach reading, writing, English grammar, arithmetic and geography. He or she must have a certificate from the Superintending School Committee to this effect. Moreover, it was the duty of the teacher, according to the state law, to

diligently impress upon the minds of the young the principles of piety and justice, a sacred regard to truth, love of country, humanity and benevolence, sobriety, industry and frugality, chastity, moderation and temperance, and all other virtues which are the ornament and support of human society.

Few are alive today who were pupils previous to 1890; therefore, little information can be given as to the individual teachers. I remember hearing my parents speak of Bion E. Gale as a good disciplinarian but who possessed a quick temper. If some act of a pupil displeased him, he was apt to pick up the nearest object at hand and throw it at the offender. As a teacher many years later, how I sometimes wished I could follow his example. It was of this same teacher that a Superintending School Committee wrote in its annual report, "His motto was, 'First order, then lessons.' This motto he put into practice most effectually, a fact to which several of the large boys can testify." An interesting statement then follows, "The scholars presented the teacher with a token of love and appreciation." This was in the Langley school district in 1883-1884.

True then (and today) there were both good and poor teachers. In this history, comments regarding the individual teachers were gleaned from the printed reports of the Superintending School Committee, and represented the opinion of one person. Fred E. Goodhue realized this, for in his report for 1885 he wrote, "I purposely omit personal criticism of the teachers, for a puff from the pen of a school committee is not always conclusive evidence of unusual ability on the part of the teacher, nor is a disparaging report from the same source always indicative of a poor school." Nevertheless, it is interesting to read these reports if for no other purpose than to compare them with what is deemed to be a good teacher today. Some words describe a school mistress as being "spunky," "energetic," "pleasant and obliging," "of noble character and a genial manner," "seems utterly incapable of embarrassment," "very thorough," "discord vanished at her presence," and on the other side, "too much sympathy for her scholars." Some of the above referred to one individual, others to several teachers. The school year 1883-1884 was the last in which teachers were mentioned individually in the report.

There appear to be two frequent criticisms of some of these early teachers—poor discipline and failure to keep or turn in the register. In the twentieth century there has been a more careful check on the latter, and it is no longer a problem. However, the matter of discipline continues. "There are needed firmness, patience, good judgment, skill and power to govern," were the words of the Superintending School Committee in 1886. How the teachers of today would applaud the following:

The failure to maintain good government was not entirely the teacher's own, neither would we consider the previous teacher alone as responsible. No school can flourish without good government and can never be easily maintained in this one school district until the teacher receives the voluntary cooperation of every parent in the district.

While the school district system existed teachers frequently moved from one district to another. A teacher might teach in one district the spring term and in another the winter term. Martha Messer, a Wilmot resident and considered to be a fine teacher, restricted her teaching to Districts No. 1 and 7. Martha J. Walker taught at least four years in four different districts, and Emma Collins, who lived at the Flat, in three districts over a period of seven years. There were five Collins sisters and they all taught in the town of Wilmot, although Ida only taught one term and this in District No. 3. Luvia taught for three years, Stella two, and Allie four years.

The annual state report for 1863-1864 gave the following statistics for that year. There were fourteen school districts with one of the schoolhouses mentioned as unfit for use. Eighteen of the teachers were females who received an average wage of $11.01 per month including board. The average wage for the male teachers was $29.20. Three teachers were considered "unsuccessful." As to the number of weeks of school, the average of the summer term was 9.63 weeks and that of the winter term 9.65 weeks.

When School Bells Rang

Subjects Taught

Research reveals that the subjects taught around 1880 were reading, spelling, penmanship, arithmetic, geography, grammar, and history. These were required in every district, but in some schools and some terms other and additional subjects were taught, probably due to the age and interests of the pupils as well as the interest and ability of the teacher. These included composition, bookkeeping, algebra, geometry, natural history, physiology, philosophy, rhetoric, and vocal music.

Latin was first taught in the summer term in 1897 and this to one pupil in the Langley School of District No. 11. Early in the twentieth century, eleven pupils in the town were enrolled in drawing. The statistical table for 1905-1906 reveals that twenty-two out of twenty-four pupils in the Flat School were taking elocution in the spring term, the same number enrolled in physical culture, and all the pupils in the school signed up for natural study. The following fall term elocution and physical culture were not continued, but vocal music was taught to all.

School Books

Until the year 1890 parents or guardians provided their children with the school books used. The state legislature in its session of 1865-1867 passed a law requiring them to do this. If they refused or neglected to do so, the cost of the books was added to the next annual tax of such a parent. For those parents who were unable to pay, books were provided at the expense of the town. We find, for example, that in 1887 books were furnished "indigent children" for the sum of $7.25.

Apparently the books in use were usually those recommended by the school committee, referred to as the "legal" books. The report of the Superintending School Committee for 1878-1879 stated that no less than eight different grammars were used in town. The following year the report spoke of a "conglomeration" of books to be found in the schools. This condition was chiefly laid to carelessness in their purchase.

To avoid confusion and thus necessitate a change in books, the state attempted to be helpful by passing laws relative to this. Any textbook, which on July 10, 1867, had been in use for less than three years, was to be continued for the term of three years from its introduction. By July, 1878, this term was increased to five years. During that time no other textbook on the same subject was to be used. An interesting exception to the above was the case in which the price of such a book was increased after its introduction.

The following books were in use as reported in 1881: *Harper's Geography, Greenleaf's Arithmetic, Harvey's Grammar, Franklin's Readers, Hilliard's Readers,* and *D. Appleton's Readers.* In the report of the following year it was announced that the *Franklin Arithmetics* would be used in 1883. At one time *Cornell's Geographies* were employed.

As might have been expected, there was criticism of the committee's choice of books and suggested changes. Evidence of this is found in the words of the Superintending School Committee which wrote,

I wish here to correct the false impression that changing school books is a remunerative occupation. For procuring the new arithmetics, distributing them to the schools, filling all of the orders, and collecting and returning the old books, I have received just and only one dollar and forty-three cents.

As to the cost of these early books, the only information is obtained from the committee report for 1883 which said,

We have arranged with publishers to furnish us with an excellent series of readers at prices within the reach of all, also a reduction in the prices of geographies had been perfected, whereby the books that cost me seventy-five cents and a dollar and a half in Concord last year, can now be furnished free of charge [to pupils] for fifty cents and a dollar and ten cents respectively.

The first year the towns were required to furnish the school books Wilmot spent three hundred dollars for this purpose. This was for the eleven school districts then in existence when summer and winter terms of school were held with an average attendance of 114 pupils. District No. 8 had an extra term with an average attendance of twenty.

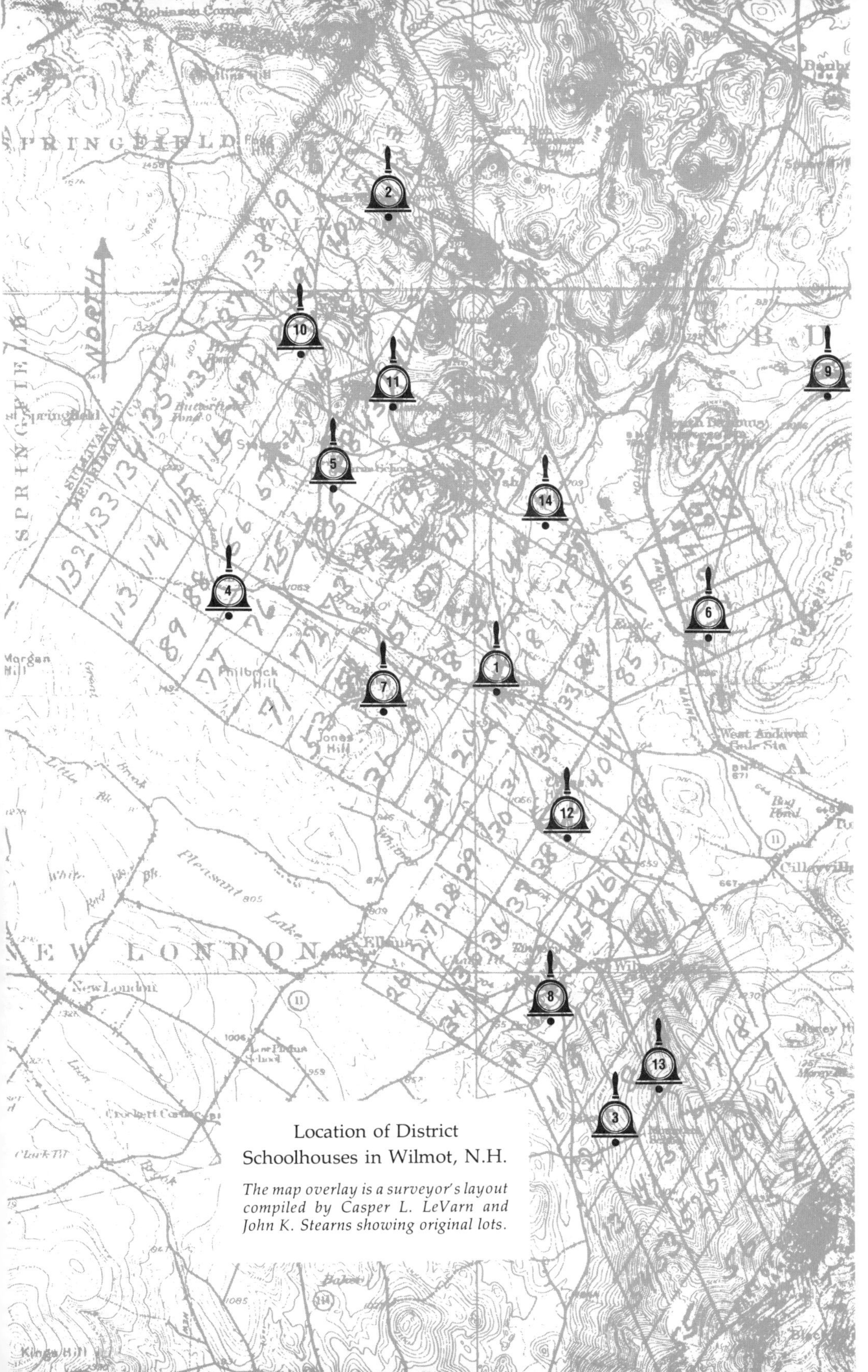

Location of District
Schoolhouses in Wilmot, N.H.

The map overlay is a surveyor's layout compiled by Casper L. LeVarn and John K. Stearns showing original lots.

The Wilmot Public Schools

District One / Center

I T WOULD SEEM that the first schoolhouse in this district was erected around 1823. In that year $10.66 was raised in school District No. 1 for the purpose of building a schoolhouse.

According to Asenath Upton Stevens the schoolhouse at the Center first stood about halfway from the Woodward place (now owned by Oliver Wilcox) to the Pingree or Pinnacle Road. This burned and a new building was erected where the present one now stands. While under construction a term of school was held in the town house, erected in 1844. When Mrs. Stevens was three years old in 1829 or 1830 she went to this first schoolhouse for half a day. She described it as being small with a fireplace, the seats all on one side, two rows for boys and the same for girls.

Sarah Teel Smith, daughter of Samuel and Ellen Clough Teel, born in Wilmot in 1848, related this account of her school in Wilmot just before the Civil War. "The building (the North District School) stood and stands now near the little river where I used to wade at recess time. The school was heated by two stoves, one at each side of the room. The desks were arranged for two, and I suppose the room would accommodate forty pupils. Of course the school was ungraded and there were almost as many classes as pupils."

Town records state that in the year 1852 the building committee of the district received $425 for building a schoolhouse. It was erected

District One class circa 1904.*

on the site of the previous one which had burned. Calvin Fisk of Wilmot sold the land for two dollars according to the deed recorded in 1861. Perhaps a description of the boundaries may be of interest:

Beginning at a stake and stones on the westerly side of the road leading by Wilmot Centre House to Danbury. Thence running westerly parallel with the school house on said lot fifteen feet north of said house, on a straight line to a stake and stones, ten feet west of said school house. Thence southerly ten feet west of said house at the north west corner on a straight line from said north west bound to the south west corner of the wood shed now standing on said land. Thence eastwardly to the before mentioned road to a stake and stones. Thence northerly on the westerly side of said road to the bound first mentioned.

When the author attended school in this building early in the twentieth century, one stepped from the entry into the schoolroom by way of two doors, the girls at the left and the boys at the right. On a shelf at the right in the entry stood the pail or stone jar of drinking

---

**BACK ROW: Flossie Dean, Paulina Arey, Grace Maxson, Clara Richmond (teacher), Viola Dean, Harland Goodhue, Leslie Gove, Clarence Prescott, Leonard Gove. FRONT ROW: Mildred Arey, Sadie Arey, Caroline Fowler, Herbert Arey, Andrew Langley, James Gove, Henry Patten, Carl Prescott.*

When School Bells Rang

District One schoolhouse flanked by Town Hall and Congregational Church about 1910.

water. There were separate toilets but they were out back and not connected to the schoolhouse. What a good excuse to get outdoors for a few minutes on a nice autumn or spring day!

The citizens in this part of the town were proud of their new schoolhouse and around 1863 at the annual meeting of the district, they voted to post a set of bylaws in some conspicuous place for the preservation of the building.

As was true in other districts there was wrangling over repairs to the building. In 1872 it was voted to raise one hundred and fifty dollars to repair the schoolhouse, part of the sum to be used for shingling, the remainder to be used inside. However, a special meeting was called for April 25th that year and it was voted *not* to raise money for that purpose, and to lay the proposed $150 item on the table. Once again the question came up the following year and this time it was voted to repair the schoolhouse and raise money for the same.

By 1878 the voters of the district agreed to raise fifty dollars for painting the school building and repairing the shed. Apparently the sum was insufficient, for the next year it was voted to raise fifty dollars to pay bills due for work and material on the woodshed, and also pay for making doors and to finish clapboarding the shed.

The appraisal value of the schoolhouse, land, and apparatus in 1886 was $205.

The Wilmot Public Schools 21

Various repairs were made from time to time. A steel ceiling was installed in 1906. Major changes had to do with heating and toilet facilities. In the early nineteen hundreds the stove was a tall round one and the contents of a metal lunch box could be heated on its top. A new stove of the box type was installed around 1922. Wood was used for fuel until a hot air oil burner replaced it in 1960 or 1961. The anteroom was converted to a cloak room by the new heating system. The left entrance only was retained.

New toilets were constructed in 1917 and $116.44 was spent for this purpose. The school superintendent, in his report for 1926-1927, wrote, "Two single unit Smith chemical toilets have been placed in the school building. By using for toilet rooms a portion of the former passageway to the shed the space available for wood is nearly doubled. It is now possible to house at one time the entire fuel supply for the year."

A further change took place about 1961 when flush toilets were installed, necessitating a septic tank and pump. A cement foundation was placed under the toilet rooms and a foundation and cement floor installed in the woodshed. Roof and walls of the woodshed were repaired and insulated, and shelving materials added to create a storeroom.

More windows were added in 1921, and combination windows installed in 1962. Window shades were added at this time. Needless to say, from time to time the floor was repaired or renewed, the walls patched and painted, and broken window glass replaced.

Until 1958 it was a building for grades one through eight in this district. This year all town pupils from grades four through eight were enrolled. In the fall of 1965 grades seven and eight were sent to school in New London, and thus 1964-1965 was the last year the school was used for pupils, marking the end of such use in the town of Wilmot.

This building now carries over its door the word LIBRARY, and as such continues to be an educational force in the town.

District Two / North Road

The history of New London contains the following item: "March 28, 1804, the settlers in the northeast district (John Clay, William Clay, Stephen Clay, Nicholas Holt, Jabez Morrill, John Russell, Robert Fowler, Samuel Fowler, Edward Buswell) were provided with schooling privileges, seventy dollars being the sum voted to build a house 30 x 16 feet. Josiah Brown was chosen to view the completed structure to see if the money was well spent."

Since this part of New London became a part of Wilmot in 1807 it would appear that the above mentioned building would be one of the town's two schoolhouses already in existence at that time.

The following excerpts from the school clerk's record are presented in diary form and thus reveal some of the early history of this, the North Road School District.

January 1, 1818 - Met at the place appointed [schoolhouse] and made choice of Timothy Flanders, Moderator and moved the meeting at Mr. Clay's. Voted that the money should be schooled out this winter by a master. Voted to give the board according to their taxes. Voted to get the wood upon free expense. Voted to have John Lowell to keep the school for eight dollars per month, to begin on Monday the 8th day of June 1816. Later the next month - Voted to have the school continue four weeks longer.

May 27, 1815 - Voted to school out half of the money this summer. Robert Fowler bid off to procure a mistress for 86 cents. Iddo Webster 64 cents per week for board.

June 29, 1815 - Voted that the school shall go on by the same mistress untill her ingagement is out which is two months.

June 7, 1816 - Voted to have a summer school. Voted to have the school as long in the summer as it will be in winter. Voted to have the school begin the 19th day of this month. Mr. John Clay bid to procure a mistress for 67 cents, at five shillings per week to keep this school. Mr. John Clay bid to board the mistress 64 cents per week.

December 7, 1816 - Voted to have the money schooled out this winter. Voted to have the school begin the first Monday of January 1817. Voted to have the money schooled out by a master. To have Halsey R. Stevens to keep the school the ensuing winter. Voted to board the master according to the scholars that each person shall send. Voted to get the wood on free expense.

January 3, 1817 - Voted to have the school keep two months from the time that it begun.

December 17, 1817 - Voted that Mr. Severnnes and Mr. E. Dean may send their children to this school with paying according to what they send. Voted to have Sarah Hobbs to teach the school this winter. Voted to give not more than one dollar per week. Voted Mr. John Clay and Lieut. Moses Currier and Capt. Iddo Webster, Committee for one year.

District Two schoolhouse on North Road around 1900.

December 24, 1817 - Voted to recall what was transacted December 17, 1817. Voted to have a school this winter.

February 4, 1818 - Voted to have the getting of school wood come out of the money at two shillings per day for each man or yoke of oxen for providing what wood shall be wanting through the school. Mr. John Clay agreed to see that the fire is built until the school is done for the ashes.

March 12, 1818 - Voted to discontinue the school. Lowell Fowler to carry the mistress home for fifty-nine cents.

June 8, 1818 - Voted to have a school as long this summer by a Mrs. as it will be next winter by a Master and give the board of a master. Mr. Morrill Currier agreed to procure a Mrs. for seventy-nine cents.

December 28, 1818 - Voted to have a school this winter, to school out all the money. Voted to give the board of master to each to board according to what one shall send. Voted Lieut. Moses Currier to produce a master to teach the school this winter. Not to give over ten dollars per month.

May 30, 1820 - Voted haul and cut wood for the fire as long as the mistress keeps the school on free cost. Mr. Thomas Currier to get the Mistress on free cost at sixty seven cents per week.

December 11, 1820 - Voted to have Mr. E. Baker to keep the school 20 days for eight dollars. Voted if Mr. E. Baker does not give general satisfaction to the District to leave the school.

October 31, 1821 - Voted that Hirum Stevens keep winter school for seven

                    When School Bells Rang

dollars per month to begin on Monday the 12th. day of November 1821.
September 1822 - Voted to have Capt. Webster get school mistress to keep a
good school. Morrill Currier bid off board at forty six cents per week.

Nothing further can be learned regarding this school district until 1838. On February third of that year there was a district meeting for the purpose of locating a schoolhouse. The site of the one which had been built before Wilmot was incorporated is not known. Apparently there was a discussion as to where the new school would be built for we read in town records that Iddo Webster and Jonathan Clay "being in the minority" felt aggrieved with the location of said house and petitioned the selectmen to appoint a committee to decide upon the proper location. The selectmen appointed Josiah Stearns, John Teel, Obadiah Clough, Asa Chapman and Calvin Fisk the committee as requested by the petition. The committee gave its report under the date of February 10, 1838, which gave its new location "In the corner of Stephen Hobb's field opposite the burying yard and adjoining John Clay's land on the road as being appropriate." That November the schoolhouse building committee received $128.25 for building the schoolhouse.

The only information pertaining to school in this district for the next few years came from some of the teachers: 1840 - Mrs. Lovina Barney and Mr. Gilbert W. Rawlins; 1841 - Miss Elisabeth H. Buswell; 1842 - Mr. Asaph Corlis and Miss Hanah G. Barney; 1843 - Lovina Barney and Gilbert Colby.

Nothing more is learned until the published report of 1878 which states that there were ten weeks of school with twenty-three scholars and that the Prudential Committee received $47.13.

A few statistics for the year ending in March, 1882, give the whole number of scholars as twenty-three, but the average daily attendance only fourteen. That was the year that the citizens, by contribution, continued the school two or three weeks after the district money had been expended. In 1907 children from the Ford, Peaslee, and Walker families, in that part of South Danbury near this district, attended the school as tuition pupils.

Apparently no school was held in this district for the years 1897-1898, 1899, 1900, 1905-1906, as the school report makes no mention of District No. 2.

Windows were added to the building in 1921-1922 and new toilets installed. Soon after the opening of the school in 1926 it was found that the attic chimney was crumbling and settling. It was then removed and an outside chimney was built at the rear of the building. This meant that the stove was then moved from the front to the rear of the room.

School was last held in 1941-1942. In 1945 the town voted to sell the building. Sixty dollars was paid for it and today it remains as a summer cottage or camp after having undergone some alterations.

District Three / Cass or Carr Hill

Previous to Wilmot's incorporation Kearsarge Gore constituted a town by itself with Kearsarge Mountain nearly in the center. It must be remembered that North Kearsarge Gore of about 6,700 acres became a part of Wilmot in 1807. This part of the gore came as far as what is designated as Wilmot Center, near what is now the residence of Thomas Voss. We find the names of Nathan Cross, Thomas Cross, Nathan Clough, Benjamin Cass, Ebenezer Fisk, Samuel Thompson, and Insley Greeley, as town officers in the North Gore, so these men can be thought of as early residents of Wilmot.

According to the *Sutton Town History*, in 1804, there were two schoolhouses in Kearsarge Gore, one being on the north side of the mountain. This would lead one to believe that there was a school building in this area which became a part of Wilmot. Its location is not known.

The following is taken from the *Sutton Town History:*

In 1829 the writer [Augusta Harvey Worthen] was employed by Deacon Insley Greeley to teach school on Cass Hill. The school was kept in the dwelling house of Benjamin Cass [J.M. Carr place] as the school house had burned. In this same house a singing-school was kept evenings by Mr. Claggett of Newport. This year was remarkable for the quantity of snow which fell.

Among the residents of the district at this time were Joseph Brown and his son Joseph, Benjamin Cass and his son Gershom B. Cass, Henry Saunders, Insley Greeley, Samuel and Noyes Cass, brothers and industrious farmers, William Morey and his sons John, Jonathan, and Levi, Samuel Kimball Esq., Widow Dudley Brown and family, and others.

Deac. Insley Greeley lived where Freeman Fellows now lives [now home of Lida Gross] and had a respectable family of several sons and daughters, Simon Greeley Esq. being the oldest son. Lieutenant Gershom B. Cass, had

When School Bells Rang

District Three class circa 1872.

a wife and two sprightly girls, was a man in his meridian, an excellent citizen, and had often been town officer. He died before thirty-six years of age. William Morey was a Revolutionary soldier and the father of a large family. [He lived near the junction of Morey Pond and Cilleville roads.] He was much respected, and by way of compliment was called Colonel. His sons John, Jonathan, and Levi lived with him. Samuel Kimball Esq. had a family of fifteen children, was a prominent man of the town, and had been frequently representative and selectman of the town. Joseph Brown [He lived on what is now the Earle Chandler place.] was a substantial farmer and his son was associated with him in cultivating the farm. Henry Saunders lived at the base of the hill, was an energetic farmer and had a wife and several children.

The above description of some of the families in this area gives a clue as to the children who attended this early school.

In 1828 there was an article in the town warrant to divide the South School District so that Samuel Carr, Gershom B. Cass, Benjamin Cass, Samuel Kimball, William Morey, Jonathan Morey, William Morey Esq., and John Morey would be in a separate district. The following year Samuel Stearns was paid one dollar to locate a school in the Cass district. This location might have been where the Cleveland cottage now stands. Mr. LeVarn states that a schoolhouse stood on the Kearsarge Reservation Road, the first corner below the tollhouse.

It was in 1855 that the voters in this District No. 3 were "aggrieved" by the location of their schoolhouse and requested the selectmen to appoint a committee to look into the matter. The committee reported that the location ought not to be changed, and the petitioners were taxed $8.34 as the cost of the hearing.

The Superintending School Committee wrote in his report for 1855-1856:

The affairs in this district relative to a schoolhouse are in a chaotic state. The house is unsound and crazy from the sills to the saddle boards. And if the old half disjointed frame with its worm eaten floor, rickety benches, shattered windows, squeaking doors, dancing at the mercy of the mountain breezes is not absolutely unsafe for scholars to congregate in its sombre ruins must be anything but inviting to the young pupil as he winds his way there on some sleety November day.

Quite a severe indictment! One is puzzled as to how a schoolhouse built about 1829 could be in such condition twenty-six years later.

We draw a blank as to information about this district between 1856 and 1878. A list of boys and girls who attended this school after 1878 include Alpha R. Atwood, Chloe I. Atwood, Luella Leavenworth, May (or Mary) B. Atwood, Maude M. Cummings, Jennie F. Fellows, William Fellows, Ina A. Fellows, Frank L. Durgin, Emily C. Durgin, Nettie Bickford, George Chase, Leroy L. Cilley, and Fred W. Chase. At one time there were seven houses on the road to Cilleville. The Atwood family lived in one of these. Seven pupils attended school in 1878 for ten weeks of school, but this district received the third largest amount of money of the thirteen districts, exceeded only by Districts No. 1 and No. 8. There were over twice as many taxpayers in this district as in District No. 13.

Teachers whose names appear between 1878 and 1892 are as follows: Ella M. Pillsbury, Stella K. Collins, Luvia M. Collins, Ida M. Collins, Emma L. Collins, Effie E. Dodge, Lucy M. Shepard, Blanche B. Whittemore, Alpha R. Atwood, and Gertrude Currier.

School was last held in this district in 1895. That year there were five scholars in the summer and fall terms.

In 1912 there was an article in the school warrant to see what action the town would take relative to the property of old school District No. 3. It was voted to sell it. The Reverend Daniel Cleveland purchased it and since his death it has remained the property of his son Irvin who maintains it as a summer cottage.

District Four / Dodge

Reports of this district before 1878 are very meager. We know that it was in existence in 1817 for the name of the collector is given. The town record states that in 1829 the committee in this district was paid for "building and repairing school house." In 1830 there were twenty resident taxpayers. When the school districts were redivided in 1843 this district was made up of Lots No. 132, 133, 134, 135, 113, 114, 115, westerly half of Lots 116 and 56, 88, 89, 75, 76, 72, 73, 74 and that part of Lot 51 owned by William Gay, the southerly halves of Lots 57 and 85, and the farms of William Smith, Thomas Brown, and Levi Savery.

In 1845 it was voted to annex this district to District No. 5 but it was separated the next year.

We do not know if, when, and where, this district kept school. In 1855 it received $31.74 in school money. The Superintending School Committee wrote of this district in 1856, "Yet without a school house, having kept in an old Blacksmith Shop this winter. The teacher and scholars labored and suffered with incredible fortitude and did as well as could be expected under the circumstances, I think one half of the time must have been taken to warm up."

In the school report for 1877-1878 this same member of the Superintending School Committee said,

District No. 4 has been without a schoolhouse for twenty-five years and today is without a legal existence, entitled to none of the school money. Whatever of the school funds have been drawn out of the town treasury the past year and expended in that district has been illegal, if I am rightly informed. Your committee understands there was no school meeting, or any attempt to have one in said district the past year. If that be true the district has lost its organization.

Does this imply that the district did have a schoolhouse at one time?

The above report resulted in action, for hearings were held as attested by expenditures listed for the year 1879-1880. One of the selectmen attended four meetings "on petition in School District No. 4," and received five dollars. The other two selectmen attended two hearings in regard to a schoolhouse in this district and received one dollar each. A schoolhouse was soon built and Sumner E. Philbrick and E.B. Dodge were paid $290.83 as the schoolhouse tax. This was

District Four schoolhouse from a photo believed to have been taken by Herbert L. Arey before 1920.

apparently the cost of building it in 1880-1881. Thus the Superintending School Committee could report, "The fall term of 1881 comfortably convened in the new school house, and the progress was very remarkable."

The appraisal value of the schoolhouse, land, etc. in 1886 was $130.79. At this time there were twenty-four resident and two non-resident taxpayers in the district.

An interesting side note: Kate Wells was paid forty cents in 1905 or 1906 "for fare of teacher from station to Mr. Dodge's."

School was last held the spring term of 1909. There was no school that fall but Miss Carrie Emerson taught the Barrett children for six weeks.

At the annual school meeting in 1926 the town voted to sell the Dodge schoolhouse and the land. One hundred dollars was received from the sale. The building is now owned by Mr. and Mrs. Charles Flanagan who, with changes and additions, have converted it into a summer home.

When School Bells Rang

District Five class in 1907.*

District Five

The school history of this area is confusing. In 1812 it was voted to have a new school district between the north and west schoolhouses. It would appear that this was District No. 5. The names of three people who taught in this district in 1818 were mentioned, and the year before it was reported that the collector for District No. 5 received $28.77, further evidence of a school. Moreover, in 1830 this was one of the larger school districts, with thirty-nine taxpayers. At this time there was no District No. 10 or District No. 11.

We do know that a schoolhouse was built around 1832 for the committee in this district was paid $142.45 in 1833 for it. Furthermore, a deed dated October 11, 1832, gives the following information:

John Moody Jr. to School District No. 5 in Wilmot, a school house lot on the west side of the road running across my land on Lot No. 46 in Wilmot and lying on the ridge about half-way from the old schoolhouse and the brook, to be five rods on the road and two rods back from the road, to contain ten square rods.

**BACK ROW: Elizabeth E. Stearns, Rose Bassett, Rodney Robie, Ralph M. Stearns. SECOND ROW: John Bassett, Louis Jacquith, Elsie J. Stearns. FRONT ROW: Ernest Tobine, Mitchell Bassett.*

The Wilmot Public Schools　　　　　　　　　　　　31

School bells ring at District Five in 1907.

Joshua Holland wrote in his reminiscences in 1916 that the schoolhouse in this district was sometimes referred to as the Kinsman schoolhouse. A Kinsman schoolhouse was also mentioned in the town record of 1831. James Clark's name was given as the teacher in 1829 or 1830. Mr. Holland added:

The schoolhouse in District 5 set in the field on the west side of the road from the North Road to the turnpike a few rods north of where the cross road from near White's Pond strikes it. Alden Youngman attended this school when he was five years of age. He came to it all one summer from his home two miles away, alone. At that time Mr. Moody lived at the house just above the field and his two boys, Moses and James, were among the scholars.

John Moody's deed to the school district speaks of "the *old* schoolhouse." This raises the interesting question as to its location. It is said that it was "in the hollow," just where is not known.

There were changes in the district from time to time. In 1843 the lots on which three men lived were severed and annexed to District No. 4. Also this same year a new district, No. 10, was created out of a part of No. 5.

Apparently the school was well thought of, as in the school report for 1882 we read, "This school which at the commencement of

When School Bells Rang

the year we considered the best in town, is composed of young scholars well-advanced in their studies who go to school to learn." Again we read the following year, "In my judgment the school still maintains its position as the pleasantess in town." Some of the scholars who attended school at about this time were children of Cyrus Langley, Joshua Holland, Horace Pedrick, Charles Trussell, and Daniel L. Thompson. It was at this time that the district was called the Buswell District.

The year 1887 was the last that school was kept in this location. It is believed that the schoolhouse was moved below the home of Minot Stearns (later burned) on the same side of the road. Henceforth it was called the Stearns School. School was no longer held after the end of June, 1925. The school building was sold in 1938 for twenty-five dollars. It became a dwelling house, now the home of Octavia Stearns. The author has pleasant recollections of being a teacher here during 1921-1923.

District Six / Eagle Pond

In its early history this was designated as District No. 11, later District No. 6. District No. 11 was in that part of the town known as New Chester. In 1820 so-called District No. 6 was made up of Lots No. 14, 15, 16, 17, 18, 19, 33, 38, 39, 40, 41, 55, 84, and 85. If one studies the map showing the original lots of the town and their approximate position it would seem that the above lots would be in the area of Wilmot Center.

Under the date of August 27, 1835, we find the following deed:

Samuel Langley to School District No. 6 a piece of land in lot no. 85 for a schoolhouse lot on the east side of the road going from Clarks Inn to Grafton and on land now occupied by Edward Currier and being where the schoolhouse fence now stands, beginning two feet north of said frame, thence south on said road three rods, thence east from said road one and half rods, to contain four and half rods of land.

At any rate, the building committee in District No. 6 was paid $52.83 and $69.10 in 1835 and 1836 for building a schoolhouse. In 1852 only $10.36 was received by the district, the smallest sum of the thirteen school districts. No further information could be found until that for the year 1878. We learn that during 1879-1880 there were two

District Six class and schoolhouse in the early 1890s.

terms of school with seven scholars each term. Family names mentioned between 1878 and 1900 included Tilton, Knowles, Morrison, Sargent, Taft, Keneston, Downes, Buswell, Thompson, Webster, Morrill, Fellows, Putney, Waldron, and Severance.

School closed in April, 1922, as there was only one pupil and she was conveyed to Cilleville.

At the school meeting in 1929 it was voted to sell the Eagle Pond schoolhouse and shed on or before May 16th of that year. The school board report for the year ending June 30, 1930, gives $47.30 received from sale of the property. The demise of the school building was noted in *The Highlander* in a Wilmot item for May 7, 1929: "James Maxfield who bought the Eagle Pond schoolhouse has torn it down. We are sorry to see the old land mark removed as the building stood on a very beautiful spot and was one of the oldest in town." When Route 4 was put through it obliterated the site.

The schoolhouse stood close to the old road which was the reason for its high windows. Since the road was later re-located, the building would have been to the right of what is now Cioffi's Garage.

                    When School Bells Rang

District No. 7 came into being about 1821. It was comprised of Lots No. 51, 52, 53, 71, 36, and one-half of Lot No. 37 owned by Jonathan Jones. Lot No. 51 was owned by Samuel Prescott. Previous to this, in 1815, the town voted that the inhabitants near Nathan Jones (in recent years known as Camp Tabor) should have the privilege of schooling out their proportion of the school money among themselves. At this time Jones had no children.

In 1837 the town voted to levy and collect the sum of $51.57 from the inhabitants of this district to repair the schoolhouse, this sum to be paid to the selectmen by the first of December that year. A town record gives the names of these inhabitants and it seems worthwhile to publish their names: Nathan Jones, Perley Messer, Daniel Emery, Willard Emerson, Obadiah Prescott, Greenleaf Prescott, Jonathan Prescott, Daniel Prescott, Samuel Prescott, Sewell Prescott. With one or two exceptions, the homes of these men are today marked only by cellar holes, dug wells, lilac bushes, and old-fashioned roses. The old stone house which Nathan Jones built and where he resided, still stands.

It is believed that the first schoolhouse burned. Supposedly it was located at the right quite far up the hill. In 1844 two inhabitants of the district asked the selectmen to appoint a committee for a "new and more equitable location" for their schoolhouse. A committee of three then appointed a time and place for a hearing. As a result the committee located the building near Asa Heath's house and on land owned by Jonathan Prescott.

A copy of the interesting deed for the land, dated August 4, 1845, reads as follows:

A certain piece of land nearly opposite Asa Heath's dwelling house and the land on which the schoolhouse now stands, and the District is to hold six feet of land for a passway to go around said house and woodsheds and when said District shall furnish another more convenient place for a schoolhouse and move the building off, it shall come into the possession of the original owner.

The price of the lot was three dollars.

One wonders what happened, if anything, to this building, for in 1853 the town paid Nathan Jones, building committee for the district, "in part $175." This would be for the schoolhouse at the foot of the hill. The map of 1858 shows it in this location.

The year 1887-1888 was probably the last year school was kept in the Prescott Hill District. Appraisal value of the building, land, etc. in 1886 was $143.94. It ranked third in value of the thirteen school districts. The town sold the schoolhouse to Newell Grace who moved it diagonally across the road and made it into his home. Since then it has been remodeled and Joe Farnum and his wife Esther now live there.

This was one school district in Wilmot which underwent few changes. In 1842 the town voted to disannex William Alexander from this district and to annex him to District No. 1, but under the date of March, 1843, the town clerk's record reads, "Voted not to include the land of William Alexander and Samuel Tenney, which is claimed by District No. 7, to District No. 1."

The district was taken to task by the Superintending School Committee in 1880:

In the summer term there were seven scholars between the ages of five and fifteen who did not attend school, and there were but eight weeks of schooling in the winter. Three years later this same committee said, "It is a fact of which perhaps not all the citizens of the district are aware, that this is not an easy school to govern."

A list of teachers during the ten year period between 1878 and 1888 includes the names of Martha M. Messer, Fred S. Langley, Lenora Walker, Laura E. Shackley, Nettie F. Currier, Clara B. Messer, Amber I. Langley, and May A. Goodhue.

District Eight / Flat

This district was organized in 1822 as the result of a petition and lay between school Districts No. 1 and 3. In 1834 the building committee received $164.09.

In 1847 there was a petition to divide it but the voters of the town turned it down. In 1850 the district lost Lots No. 11, 26, 27, 34, 35, 36, 37, 42, 100, and all that part of Lot No. 44 lying west of Otis Jones' mill pond, and all of No. 43 that Benjamin R. Andrews owned. This area was to form a new district, No. 13.

This same year a number of the legal voters in District No. 8 were aggrieved by the location of their schoolhouse. Where this site was is

When School Bells Rang

District Eight class circa 1908.

not known. An appointed committee chose the new location on "Lot No. 44 at southwest corner of said lot on the north side of road leading from Wilmot Flat by William Pillsbury's house and about opposite of the Burying Yards at or near a stake and stones." The cost of the hearing by the selectmen was to be paid by the district, taxed at $5.50.

Thomas Peaslee of Wilmot, cordwainer, sold the land to District No. 8 for eighty-five dollars. It is described and bounded as follows:

To commence at the Northwest corner of land of Peter McKenzie's land and on the East side of the road leading from Wilmot Flat to Sutton, and running Northerly on said road ten rods to a stake and stones, thence Easterly to run parallel with said McKenzie's North line to the Pond, thence Southerly on said Pond ten rods to said McKenzie's land; thence Westerly on said McKenzie's North line to the bound begun at, to contain by estimation three fourths of an acre be the same more or less.

This deed was recorded June 9, 1851. It would seem that this was a high price for land in those days.

There was much dispute over the question of the schoolhouse as to whether or not the old one should be sold and if so a new one erected. The vote of the men in that district at their March meeting seems unreasonable as they "Voted to sell the old schoolhouse on Saturday next," *but* "Voted not to build a new school house or to raise money or take any measure thereof.'' There were district meetings in June, July, and September. In September the vote was to repair the old schoolhouse and fifty dollars was raised for that purpose. The selectmen were to be a committee to make repairs. Whether repairs were made is not known, probably not.

At a meeting in April of the following year the question was finally resolved as the vote not to build was reconsidered. The old schoolhouse was sold to Simon Greeley for $56. This time the vote was to build and a committee was chosen to "fix" upon a location and procure a plan for the building.

Later that same month it was voted to raise $300 that year for the schoolhouse. The treasurer was to hire money to complete the building, not to exceed $350. Moreover, the building was to be finished by the first day of October. Naturally a committee of three was appointed to superintend the erection of the building.

Progress could then be reported for in seven days the committee brought in a report. The site chosen was on the south end of Thomas Peaslee's pond lot adjoining Peter McKenzie's. This would seem to be the location of the present building. Benjamin Cilley built the schoolhouse and furnished all material for $575. George Shepard and Daniel Hazen built the shed for $49. Extra graining of inside doors and desks was $2.25. The total sum expended for land and buildings was $725.43; money received from the town was $224.98.

Now that the schoolhouse was built the people of the district were proud of it. In October that year concern was shown about its care, for at a district meeting they "Voted that the teacher take all pre-measures not to have the school house or seats cut or marked or in any way disfigured, or characters drawn on the outside of the house or about the shed or back house." If defacement were to occur it was to be reported to the Prudential Committee. The following Saturday evening ladies and gentlemen of the district were invited to attend an adjourned meeting "at early candle light," at which time W.W. Flanders would give an address.

This same month it was decided to class the school, with scholars under twelve years of age to go into the junior department, and all over the age of twelve go into the senior department.

The following year, 1851, it was decided to fence the schoolhouse lot and fifty dollars was raised to pay for this. In 1867 the question of the fence came up and the Prudential Committee was authorized to build a substantial one and put in a new gate. Three

When School Bells Rang

years later members of the district voted to sell the stone posts in front and at the rear of the schoolhouse and repair the fence each side of the lot. Tied in with the matter of fencing is an interesting item of business for 1855, "Voted that Daniel M. Hazen be a committee to take charge of the schoolhouse yard and keep out all four-footed animals."

Although it was voted to paint the schoolhouse in 1862 all was not serene in the district, for the Prudential Committee that year reported a balance of $17.29 saying, "The reason why I did not school out the rest was that I considered the school of no benefit to the district." One wishes he knew the "why" of this remark.

Apparently there was a need for meeting places in this end of town, for in 1855 the district voted to open the schoolhouse for evening writing schools, singing schools, public lectures, and lyceums as wanted. Each society occupying the schoolhouse for purposes mentioned was to choose one of their number to open the schoolhouse and to see to the fire. Whether advantage was taken in using the building is not known but in 1872 the Prudential Committee was instructed to let the schoolhouse for any schools which in its judgment were of benefit to the district. That year seventy-five cents was received from Pierce and Fellows for a writing school, and the next year "received of Wm. Fellows for wood for writing school seventy-five cents." There must have been some dissatisfaction with the use of the building, for when the question came up again the district decided that the schoolhouse was to be used only for common school and economical purposes.

Twenty-six years after the schoolhouse was built it was remodeled by putting it all into one schoolroom with necessary closets. Three years later, in 1880, forty dollars was raised to repair and paint the building. S.P. Hall was paid $65 for the schoolhouse tax. At an adjourned meeting twenty-five dollars was raised to repair the underpinning, to grade around the schoolhouse, to batten the house floor underneath, and to repair the shed.

The appraisal value in 1886 was $272.66, the largest sum of all the thirteen districts.

After this date repairs and improvements to the building were made from time to time. Windows were added and later screened. One year the stove was moved to the northwest corner and jacketed. Two stoves were purchased in 1936. A big change took place around 1949 when the fuel was changed from wood to oil, electric lights and new septic toilets installed at a total cost of $974.99.

This was the first one-room school in the union to have its own water supply. It was a hand pump located in the corridor of the school building. The teacher, Mrs. Lorraine Cadoo, and her pupils, plus many citizens of the community raised the funds necessary for the project. This took place during the school year of 1927-1928.

In 1958 only the first three grades in town attended the Flat School. The year 1968 marked the last that school was held in the building.

District Nine / East Wilmot

This area was not a part of Wilmot when the town was incorporated in 1807. It was a part of New Chester and by petition and an act of the legislature it was annexed in December, 1832. Adding about thirty thousand acres, it was thereafter spoken of as East Wilmot.

The deed to the schoolhouse lot registered under the date of November 2, 1835, reads as follows:

Jonathan Buck of Wilmot in the County of Merrimack and state of New Hampshire for one dollar to School District No. 9 in said Wilmot, a certain piece of land for a schoolhouse lot situated in Wilmot aforesaid in that part formerly New Chester and is a part of Lot No. 93 in the fourth division of lots and is the same where the schoolhouse now stands. Bounded as follows, viz. to extend on the road fifty feet and to run back thirty feet from the road wall and the west line of said land, is to be six feet to the west end of the schoolhouse.

Fifty-six dollars was paid the building committee so apparently the schoolhouse was built in 1834. Mr. LeVarn, in his *Early History of Wilmot*, states that the schoolhouse was located about three miles up the New Canada road on the first fork. As far as the existence of this district is concerned it ended for Wilmot in 1887 when a part of East Wilmot was sold to Danbury. We do know that the appraised value in 1886 was $48.32.

We draw a blank as to information on this district until the year 1879 when we learn that Cora I. Sargent and Clara M. Farnum taught here. At one time there were nineteen scholars. The roll of honor for various years reveals the names of some of the pupils in this school: Pearl C. Whittemore, Lucy Severns, Henry M. Farnum, Idella K. Farnum, Bertha M. Farnum, and Millie F. Reed. The names of W.H.H.

When School Bells Rang

Peabody and J.M. Bean are found in the list of Prudential Committees giving another clue as to who lived in this community.

District Ten

When the school districts were redivided in 1843 District No. 10 was created. Previous to this date the citizens of this area were in District No. 5. This new district consisted of

that part lying north and west of the farms of Asa Chapman and Samuel Stearns and containing the following names and number of lots: Andrew Langley part of Lot No. 9 and part of 8, Samuel Langley half of Lot No. 9, Samuel Thompson Lot No. 10, Asa Chapman part of Lot No. 45 and part of No. 18, Henry Tewksbury part of Lot No. 119, Stephen Tewksbury part of Lot No. 119, Asaph Corlis half of Lot No. 118, Bailey Corlis part of Lot No. 138, Nathaniel G. Rollins part of Lot No. 138 and part of Lot No. 137, Andrew Langley 2nd part of Lot No. 138.

By comparison with some of the other districts it led an untroubled existence as to its boundaries. At one time the farm where Richard P. Stearns lived was disannexed from District No. 11 and added to this district. This was the only change which could be found.

Henry Tewksbury deeded the schoolhouse lot to District No. 10 "as long as we may want to occupy for the same for a schoolhouse." The deed was dated April 26, 1845, and pinpoints the location of the building, "on the west side of the road running by my house to Col. Samuel Thompson's and about 15 rods west of my old grist mill to a stake and stones, thence 4 rods in front running back to stake and stones two rods and a half, to contain one six-tenths of an acre." Henry Tewksbury lived up the hill on a farm on the right hand side of the road, later known as the George Tewksbury place. The Colonel Thompson place was on the road going to the right of the North Wilmot Church. By vote of the district Mr. Tewksbury was given five dollars for the land.

The district voted that the schoolhouse be built like the North Road schoolhouse. Men of the district agreed to meet together and level the spot and put up the frame without a tax. Underpinning was to be of split stone on the front and ends, the back of common stone. There was to be a good doorstep and a porch. It was decided to sell the erection of the building to the lowest bidder, to be divided into small jobs. Interesting figures reveal the following: Samuel Langley, the underpinning for $6.95; Bailey Corlis, the boarding and window frames at $11.70; Daniel Richards, shingling and coveing $7.80; Nathaniel Rollins, clapboarding, planed casings, door frame and door stool at $16.90; glueing of nine windows with sash primed and window over the door bid off to Samuel Thompson at $12.45, also stove and funnel fitted for use, $13.25; laying floors and seats to Asa Chapman at $18.25; ceiling up to the windows, batting and plastering front and inside doors, to Andrew Langley at $15.00; painting and door lock to Andrew Langley, bid off at $8.00. Naturally a committee of three was elected to examine the work, said committee consisting of Samuel Thompson, Andrew Langley, and Daniel Richards.

We have a clear picture of the progress this district made through the excellent records kept by Daniel Richards, the first district clerk. It was at the March 2nd meeting in 1843 that the district voted to build a schoolhouse to be finished on or before the 20th of the following September. This year there were seven adjourned meetings, and for the first time a meeting took place in the new schoolhouse on October 14th.

One term of school of fourteen and one-third weeks was held the first year with Miss Mary Kinsman as teacher. For this she received $21.50. The district allowed tuition pupils from outside the area if they paid twelve and one-half cents per week and a proportion of the wood and board of the teacher. The Prudential Committee's report for the year ending March 11, 1844, contains this item: "Received from Elijah Morril for tuition 12½c." The district received $18 raised by the town and $3.47 from the Literary Fund, leaving cash on hand of $0.09.

In March, 1847, the district voted to erect a wood house 12'x10' with 7' posts. The "boddy" of the house was to be double boarded, the roof boarded and shingled. It was to have a plank floor with the south end of the building made into a "necessary" 4' wide, painted in the middle with a door in each part and a door in the wood apartment. Lowest bid was for $14.86. The building was to be finished by the first of November.

After the school was established the district meetings followed the usual pattern as to how the wood would be obtained, when the terms of school would open, whether to hire a male or female teacher, and provision for minor repairs to the school building. One item of interest is that in 1853 "the district voted their willingness to have their children under the control of the teacher going and returning

When School Bells Rang

District Ten schoolhouse with North Wilmot Church in background as they looked in the late 1890s.

from school." Later it was voted to have an inside lock on the outside door. Another item states that the district voted to exclude from the schoolhouse all meetings except the preaching of the gospel.

A hint as to the first taxpayers in the district is obtained from an item under the date of May 9, 1845:

We the undersigned names have received our shares in full of the old schoolhouse in District No. 5: Samuel Thompson, Stephen Tewksbury, Henry Tewksbury, Daniel Richards, Deac. Andrew Langley, "Blacksmith" Andrew Langley, Asa Chapman, Nathaniel G. Rollins, Samuel Langley, Asaph Corlis, Bailey Corlis, Isiah Langley.

The sum of $17.77 was divided according to the proportion of tax each paid for building the schoolhouse in District No. 10. The sum each received varied from $0.43 to $3.35.

The first record book of the district clerk ends with the year 1866. No further records could be found until 1878 when the Superintending School Committee had a report of the town schools published in the town report. We learn that this year the district had sixteen weeks of school with twenty-three scholars. The following year it ranked third of the thirteen districts as to the number of scholars.

There were twenty-nine different teachers listed in the period between 1843 and 1866. The Superintending School Committee made two interesting comments regarding one or two of the young teachers sometime after 1878:

This school is slightly inclined to insubordination and as the teacher was young they took advantage . . . Miss Nellie M. Ross came here with a purpose to do well and was generally successful. Near the close of the term a disturbance arose in which the teacher was charged with inflicting too severe punishment, but even if such may have been the case, Miss Ross should not bear all the blame, as a feeling was apparent among some of the parents which would be quite likely to mislead a young teacher, but which one of experience might apprehend and over-rule without difficulty.

Another teacher by the name of Clara Ross, not to be confused with Nellie M. Ross, taught the winter term of eleven weeks in 1880-1881. In the words of the Superintending School Committee:

When this term commenced the school was in the worst condition of any in town, at the close it ranks among the first. The scholars not only showed improvement in study, but were successfully taught to be polite to each other and respectful to their teacher. To the untiring energy of the teacher belongs the credit of effecting the greatest school reform during the year in town.

The Superintending School Committee wrote in 1883: "We understand that but for a mistake in the returns this dilapitated old shell of a schoolhouse would have given place to a new and comely structure." One can speculate as to the mistake, but regardless, the appraisal value in 1886 was only $9.94 which gives some indication of the condition of the building. School was last held in this building in District No. 10, or the Langley District, in 1887 or 1888. It is said that it was taken down and the lumber used for a hen house. In 1897 three schoolhouses in town were sold for thirty-nine dollars and this might have been one of them. Thus endeth this school but not its influence on former pupils who attended here.

                                        When School Bells Rang

This district was formed in 1843, the same year as District No. 10. It included Lots No. 6, 11, 12, 13, 14, 15, 42, 44, 49, and that part of 43 and 45 owned by John White.

It was not until September, 1845, that the legal voters located the schoolhouse "on James G. White's and John White's land on the west side of the road leading from John Teel to said Whites." Here again the schoolhouse in District No. 2 served as a model, for it was voted to build the house the same "bigness," to paint it the same color, and to get a stove like that of the district. Different parts of the construction were "sold" to various individuals. The following April it was voted to take enough of the surplus to build a woodshed to be finished by the first of December.

Repairs on the building were made from time to time. In 1859 it was voted to shingle the shed with shaved shingles and to put on boards "if any are found rotten." Ten years later it was decided to remove and "fit up" the schoolhouse and shed and to secure a new location. Fifty dollars were raised for the entire project. Curtis Langley was paid $10.00 for the land and C.M. Stewart received $26.50 for moving the buildings. As reported at the district meeting the total cost of the undertaking was $51.60, the amount of money received was $51.61, leaving a balance on hand of one cent. By 1874 more repairs were necessary and twenty-five dollars was raised for this.

The usual business took place at the district meetings. In 1862 it was voted to receive scholars from other districts at ten cents per week. It was at this meeting that it was decided to sell the board of the teacher to J.L. Teel for 94 cents per week, but then the issue was reconsidered and it was voted that the teacher board herself.

Here again little is known about the school until 1878. Some of the teachers in the early period were Mercy (or Mary) E. Gifford, Ellen Barney, Sarah Currier, and Harriet Langley. One winter term twenty-three scholars were enrolled but the average attendance was thirteen. Statistics reveal that there were two terms of school in 1881-1882 with seventeen scholars. On the roll of honor for that year were Bert Langley, Eddie Langley, Clara Langley, Grace Langley, Minnie Langley, Mattie Langley, Earnest Brown, Eddie Joice, Sumner Philbrick, Bertha Atwood, and Cora White.

School continued in this district until the end of June, 1903. There were seven scholars the last year. The building remained empty

District Eleven schoolhouse in the early 1900s.

until 1920-1926 when it was reopened and the Stearns school closed. Now it was spoken of as the Langley schoolhouse, sometimes it was called the Pond School as it was near White Pond. Previous to the reopening the woodshed was moved and connected to the schoolhouse with an entrance into the schoolhouse. Sills and floors were replaced in both schoolhouse and shed. More windows were added, walls and ceiling refinished with wallboard. One could enter the chemical toilet room directly from the schoolroom. The warmed coatroom was provided with a wet sink and stone water cooler. Movable chair desks and new blackboards were installed. The entire cost of this renovation was $642.39.

By 1933-1934 the school was no longer needed and was again closed, this time for good. At a special school meeting in June, 1946, it was voted to sell the schoolhouse and to set the price at $150. Robert Stewart purchased the building and made it into his home.

When School Bells Rang

District Twelve / Cross Hill

This was a district which suffered birth pangs. In 1843 a committee of one from each of the eleven districts was chosen at the March meeting "to alter, divide, make anew and define the limits of each district and report for action of the town at an adjourned meeting." This was quite an assignment! At the adjourned meeting held the next month it was voted "*not* to accept of the Committee Report as reported." Instead the voters proceeded by acting on the report of the committee but taking up the districts separately.

Apparently the committee divided the districts by lots without boundaries, for three days later thirteen petitioners, most of whom appeared to be from District No. 5, requested the selectmen to "divide the town into convenient School Districts, define their limits, boundaries, and cause a record thereof to be made by the Town Clerk."

The lengthy description of the new District No. 12 is not given here, but it was made up of Lots No. 28, 29, 30, 31, 38, 39, 46, 47, 48, part of 21, and one-half of 30. The next year, 1844, there was an article in the warrant to abolish this district, "it being formed contrary to a vote of the town," but the town voted against this.

Little is known about the schoolhouse in this district. It was located at the foot of Cross Hill on the left-hand side of the road going from Wilmot Center to Wilmot Flat. In 1870 twenty-five dollars was received for a schoolhouse tax which would indicate that repairs were made to the building. It was in the year 1880-1881 that the Superintending School Committee spoke of the poor condition of the schoolhouse and the small amount of money this district received.

Possibly this comment accounted for the fact that in 1883 the district received $26.08 as a schoolhouse tax. The appraised value in 1886 was $74.36. No records available provide clues as to school in this district between 1843 and 1878. For the school year 1877-78 there were fourteen weeks of school with eighteen scholars. The following year there were ten weeks of school and the attendance had dropped to fourteen. Attendance fluctuated from year to year, and in 1881 the enrollment for the fall term of eleven weeks was nine boys and six girls. It was in 1883 that there were two terms of school taught by different teachers, and the Superintending School Committee reported, "Let it be understood that some of the scholars in this district are not overburdened with a zeal for knowledge and that this is no place for a teacher to win laurels."

There was no school in this district between 1887-1888 and in 1891 there were summer and fall terms of ten and twelve weeks respectively with an average attendance of twelve and nine. The following year was the last year school was held in the Cross Hill District. According to Arthur Thompson the building was sold to Arthur Clark on Pancake Street and became a part of his carriage shed, the end nearest to the house. We know that in 1897 three schoolhouses were sold for thirty-nine dollars, perhaps this included the one on Cross Hill.

District Thirteen

This district wore the colorful name of "Under The Hill" and certainly it had a much blurred, colorful beginning. In 1849 the town voted to have a new school district embracing the territory described in the petition of Joseph Chase and others, to be known as District No. 13, but the above vote was rescinded the following year.

In 1856 seven men petitioned the town to create School District No. 15, passing over the number 13. Their request was denied, but not daunted, this same group of men made a like petition in 1858 but calling the new district No. 13. This time the district was established and money received for the first time. The area it encompassed may be found in *The Early History of Wilmot* by Casper L. LeVarn.

A report of the Superintending School Committee in 1878 suggested that Districts No. 3 and 13 which formerly constituted one district should be reunited. The report further said, "The schoolhouses stand in full view and within rifle shot of each other. Both of the old houses would make one good house and would have to be moved not more than forty rods on an old highway discontinued by abandonment, to meet on the same ground." His recommendation was not carried out.

The appraisal value in 1886 was $124.12, thus ranking it the sixth highest of the thirteen schools in existence at that time. There were twelve taxpayers plus two non-resident taxpayers in the district.

Some repairs were made to the building in 1879 and 1881 as evidenced by the fact that the district received $17.75 and $16.50 respectively.

Apparently 1886 or 1887 was the last year school was held in this district, and this for only one term. What became of the building is not known, but the Mountain School was built on its location in 1911.

District Fourteen

Very little is known about this district. It was formed in 1850 by setting off a part of District No. 8, and was made up of Lots No. 40, 41, 46, 55, 84, 16, 17, and parts of 39, 15, and 42, originally in New London. Thus it would extend from the Washington Morrison place on Teel Hill to the south end of Eagle Pond on the west side, and from the junction of Richard Road to Lucien Morrill's corner.

In 1852 the building committee received $71.29 for a schoolhouse. This year the town allotment was $11.61 and the interest and fund money was $3.58, which with the exception of District No. 6 was the smallest sum received by any of the thirteen districts.

It is said that the schoolhouse was located on the road between Lucien Morrill's place (Fred LeVarn's) and the Town Poor Farm, on the left-hand side of the road. A map of 1858 shows a school in this area. Families who lived in this vicinity included those of Jesse Waldron, Hiram Buswell, Joseph K. Wallace, Thomas Putney, Baruch C. Clough, Samuel Waldron, and Charles Trumball.

In 1876 the district was dissolved and the schoolhouse and property sold. It was annexed to Districts No. 1, 6, and 11.

Mountain School

This was the last schoolhouse to be built in Wilmot. The school warrant printed in the town report for 1911 under article 10 reads, "To see if the district will vote to build a school house on Kearsarge mountain." The word "on" is misleading for it was built on the site of the old one in District 13, or Under The Hill. Five hundred dollars was appropriated for the structure and it was built by Jerry Morey for this sum.

School opened in the fall of 1912 with nine pupils. Around 1922 new toilets were provided and the barbed wire fence adjoining the school yard was replaced by plain wire. A year later a coat of paint was

The Mountain schoolhouse in 1919.

applied to the outside. In 1924 this school, sometimes called District No. 13, was closed after the ninth week and the four Wilmot pupils were sent to the Flat school.

The number of school age pupils in this area increased a few years later and at the annual school meeting in 1933 it was voted to repair the schoolhouse and maintain a school in the building. The cost of altering the building was $351.76, and fifteen pupils were registered that year. The year 1943-1944 marked the end of this school's existence. At the regular school meeting in March, 1946, it was voted to sell the school building with the school board to confer with the Selectmen to determine and fix a price for the building. Three years later it was sold to Emery S. Bailey for six hundred dollars and he converted it into his dwelling.

Individuals who taught in this school included Edna B. Dodge, Eva M. Currier, James B. Morey, Lena B. Morey, Elsie Bunn, Isabel Morey, Doris True, Celia A. Dean, Beth S. Swett, Ellen J. Hines, Della Fifield, Theresa Atwood, and Lorraine Cadoo.

Pupils included Lida Howard, Wilbur Howard, Henry Rayno, Maurice Rayno, Edna Rayno, Roland Morey, Bernice Morey, Marion Phelps, Edith Morgan, Viola Morgan, John French, Doris Thompson, and Ruth Huntoon.

                                 When School Bells Rang

Secondary Education Outside Wilmot

Note should be taken of some of the opportunities for secondary education which existed at one time for the youth of Wilmot. Andover Academy, in the adjoining town of Andover, opened in August, 1848, and discontinued as such in 1854. One hundred and eight pupils were enrolled the first term, seven of these were from Wilmot, six girls and one boy. A total of forty-six young men and women from Wilmot enrolled during the existence of the school. Dave Flanders, Abby C. Saunders, and Martha F. Saunders attended for three years, while most of the others enrolled for only one year. Warren Langley was eighteen years old when he attended, his sister Harriet, fifteen.

There were two departments of study: English and Ancient and Modern Languages. Most of the pupils from Wilmot enrolled in the English department, six enrolled in both. Tuition was three dollars per quarter for common branches, three dollars and fifty cents for higher English branches and language and two cents per week for incidental expenses. There were four terms of twelve weeks each.

In 1899 the legislature passed a law that any boy or girl living in a town which did not maintain a high school might attend an approved high school with his tuition paid by his home town or district. Thereafter most of those from Wilmot attended Proctor Academy in Andover, Colby Academy in New London, or Franklin High School.

The Kearsarge School of Practice

The Kearsarge School Of Practice

T HE STORY of Wilmot's schools
must certainly include the history
of the Kearsarge School of Practice. Although it cannot be proved, it is
believed that originally this school had its start in Elkins in what is
now the Masonic Hall opposite the village store.

In 1876 Mrs. Isaac Youngman became interested in the school.
She purchased the land and buildings at Wilmot Center from James B.
Stearns and Baruch Clough, renovated the main building and sold it to
the Rev. John H. Larry for five dollars. Old deeds show that between
1840 and 1852 a building was on this site, whether or not it was the
building which now stands, or only a portion of it, is not known.

The first year the school was opened in 1876-1877 a circular
published by the Larry Press called the school the "School of Practice."
Perhaps the word Kearsarge was not added until 1884 when the school
was incorporated as the Kearsarge School of Practice. There were nine
incorporators who also constituted the board of trustees. Members of
this board were Isaac B. Youngman, Hannah Youngman, James
Stearns, Charles F. Trussell, John M. Carr, Sumner E. Philbrick,
Charles H. Thompson, Maria H. Thompson, and Luther M. Keneston.
In 1911 the number of board members was reduced to five.

Site of the school is pinpointed by a deed in 1884 whereby
Hannah Youngman and her husband Isaac B. Youngman,

in consideration of one dollar paid by Kearsarge School of Practice Association of Wilmot have granted, bargained, and sold a certain piece of land with the buildings thereon situated in said Wilmot bounded and described as follows. Beginning at the Northely corner of Ebben Farnum's land, thence southerly on said Farnum's west line to the Cimetry, thence on the North line of the Cimetry to the Highway, thence on said Highway to the 4th N.H. Turnpike to the first mentioned bound, estimated to contain two acres the same more or less. Said premises being conveyed for School purposes to said Association in the interest of the Youth of said Wilmot. Reserving the use of the land our natural lives that's not necessary for use or enjoyment of said building. Also reserving the water as it's now conveyed to us, to the benefit of the place forever, not to exceed half of the fountain head at any time.*

Hannah and Isaac Youngman and Calvin Fisk were the chief benefactors of the school. Calvin Fisk in his will written in 1882 gave the residue of his estate "to the support of a term of Select school in the Fisk Hall at Wilmot Center or the interest of the same yearly forever." The sum is believed to have been about $1,300. Mr. Youngman, in his will dated 1889, left three thousand dollars to the school, and Hannah's will written nine years later left six thousand dollars as a school fund. Both Mr. and Mrs. Youngman made provision in case of the destruction of the building, saying "then it may be schooled in next best place at Wilmot Centre or until another is provided." These benefits for the "Youth of Wilmot" continue today.

The first school circular dated 1876-1877 lists Mr. and Mrs. Youngman, Mr. and Mrs. Calvin Fisk, and Mrs. William P. White as having contributed one hundred dollars and upward to the school. Five donors were listed who gave twenty-five dollars or more, and twenty-eight individuals who gave ten dollars and under. These figures indicate the interest taken by the citizens of Wilmot.

In 1876-1877 the Kearsarge School of Practice was in session with Professor Larry, as he was affectionately called, as its principal. Not known is the number of years Mr. Larry served in this capacity.

Fortunately a circular gives a good picture of the school's first year. In addition to being principal Mr. Larry taught mathematics, natural science, and other subjects. Mr. L.B. Hampton was the instructor in bookkeeping and penmanship, and Olive J. Hobbs instructor in piano and organ.

---

*Original spelling

     When School Bells Rang

Kearsarge School of Practice in the early 1900s.

There is so much of interest in this circular that we believe it merits space in this school history. As to its location,

The School of Practice is located on elevated ground, having five mountain views to the south and east, and shielded on the north by a chain of lofty hills. This situation was chosen by the proprietor with especial reference to its healthfulness and the freedom of the village from debasing influences.

Naturally parents would be concerned as to the moral atmosphere of the school. They could be reassured by this paragraph:

The school stands high in moral tone. Almost daily instruction in Christian morals serves, without harsh rules, to guard the students from bad habits and uncouth manners. It is our desire to develop true manhood and womanhood as well as to train and discipline the mind. Though unsectarian religiously, and independent politically, the principal believes it a part of his duty to teach the young to love their God and their country, to think and to act from pure and unselfish motives.

This first year certificates were granted to those scholars whose deportment was satisfactory and who had passed examinations in those branches with which a district school teacher should be familiar. A certificate was also given to those who had completed the business course. Each scholar in bookkeeping was furnished merchandise with

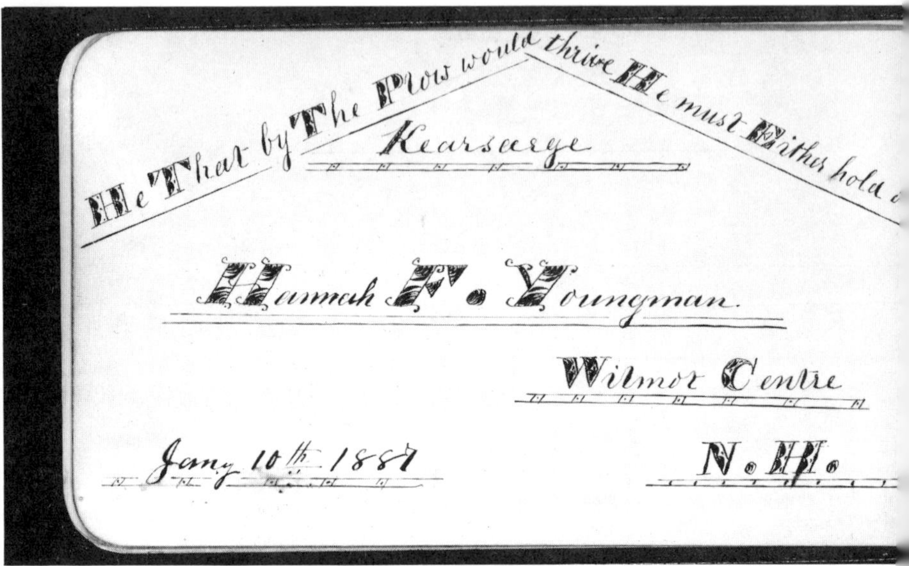

cash for capital and given a business to manage. The business course included bookkeeping, arithmetic, penmanship, philosophy, English analysis, elocution, spelling, historical readings, and geography.

Ordinary tuition was five dollars per term, common tuition, an additional two dollars; penmanship, one hour lesson daily, one dollar; higher English branches each, an extra fifty cents. Room and board could be obtained in the school itself, rent per week was about twenty-five cents, board per week, "everything found," was three dollars. Table board in the Hygeia Club was about one dollar and twenty-five cents. (What could this club have been?)

There was a preparatory or model class under the supervision of Mrs. Larry. The reason for its existence was explained in these words:

The principal wishing to educate his own children, receives into his school young pupils who are taught orally to a considerable extent and trained, as he believes all scholars should be, in good morals and gentle manners as well as in their studies.

Nineteen were enrolled in this class the first year, sixteen from Wilmot and one each from West Andover, Newport, and Wakefield,

                                    When School Bells Rang

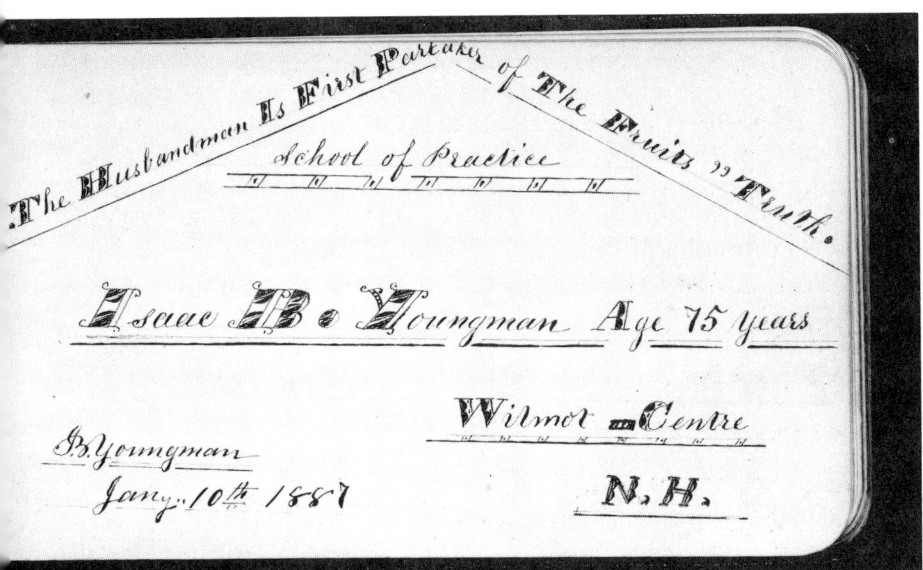

*Cursive inscription of Isaac and Hannah Youngman in autograph book believed to·
have belonged to Joshua Holland in 1887.*

Massachusetts. A research of their birth records revealed that the average age was ten years.

We know the students who attended this first year for their names were printed in the circular with the town in which they lived. The list contains sixty-three names. Twenty were from Wilmot Center, eight from North Wilmot, and nine from the Flat. In addition two from West Andover and Londonderry, three from Springfield and Enfield, four from Scytheville (Elkins), six from North Sutton, and one each from Andover, New London, Danbury, Grafton, Canaan, and Wells, Maine. More boys than girls were enrolled, as perhaps one might expect. In its most flourishing days it had over one hundred students, more than attended Colby Academy during the same period.

No more is known about the school until 1884-1885. Luther M. Keneston was then principal and taught mathematics and languages. There was also a woman principal, Miss Lill E. Philbrick. She had charge of the primary department and sciences. Miss Addie E. Babbitt was the instructor in instrumental music and Mr. A.J. Buswell that of vocal music.

This year there were three terms of school, twelve weeks each, opening dates being September 2nd, December 2nd, and March 3rd. There were three courses of study: Classical (designed to fit young men to enter college); Academic or Ladies Collegiate (similar to classical except French and other studies substituted for Greek); and English (to prepare young men and women for the active pursuits of business life). The cost was six dollars per term, but less for Wilmot pupils. A telegraph line had been constructed from the school building to West Andover and the cost of studying telegraphy was six dollars.

This circular gives information as to what a student could expect in regard to the operation of the school. There was still grave concern about the health, moral, and intellectual training of the scholars as evidenced by the paragraphs which follow.

Students are expected to be present at the devotional exercises of the school and to attend a Bible exercise once a week at such times as the teachers shall direct. Those remaining in the village will be required to keep study hours Saturday evening and attend church on the Sabbath. . .

A weekly record of deportment is kept and sent to the student's parents at the close of the term. Violations of school regulations, or departures from the propriety becoming persons who have arrived at years of discretion, will be demerited separately. When these demerits have reached ten, they will be reported to parents, when they amount to twenty the student will be dismissed from school.

Some of the present generation will be aghast on hearing of the regulations: "All walks, rides, and visiting between the students of the Male and Female Departments are prohibited except by special permission from the President and Lady Principal." (Does the word President refer to the principal or to the President of the Board of Trustees?)

Young ladies are not expected to receive calls on the Sabbath, or visit away from their boarding places during term time, without being previously excused by the Lady Principal. No student is allowed to leave town, or visit other villages in this town without special permission from the proper authorities.

Under Amusements we find, "Scholars will *At Proper Times*, be allowed the free use of ball and bat, hammock, swings, and croquet set, and ladies who wish to ride can have the use of a horse and saddle for a small compensation."

     When School Bells Rang

The physical well-being of pupils was in part taken care of by these statements,

The school building is always well warmed in winter, and is well supplied with excellent water. Here is also ample room for the storage of wood and other articles. Every accommodation of a good home is so arranged that scholars rooming in the building need not step out of doors. Scholars who board at home will be allowed a warm waiting room and a right to all the privileges of the house. A team connected with the school will be used for the free conveyance of scholars who live in and about the village to and from school on stormy days.

The physical plant consisted of a three-story main building with a back hallway connecting it to a barn at the left. A cupola on top of the barn held the school bell. This bell was purchased many years later by Mrs. Bessie Kurth and installed on the premises of the old Graney home on Cross Hill. A small captain's walk (or similar structure) was on top of the roof of the main building. It is there no longer but was in place for some time after the annex was taken down. A porch extended on two sides of the building. Attached to the right of the main building was a two-story annex known as Fisk Hall. When this was removed is uncertain, but it was sometime after 1904. The headmaster's apartment was on the first floor of the main building, the second floor was used for boarding pupils, with the classroom on the third.

A kitchen and dining room were on the first floor of the annex with rooms for self-boarding pupils on the second floor. Seldon Tewksbury of North Wilmot and his sister Gertrude attended school one year, probably in 1883 or 1884, and boarded themselves. Seldon was sixteen or seventeen years old at the time and his sister a year or two younger. In his memoirs he wrote, "Had an old kitchen stove in my room to cook potatoes on. Also toasted bread on the cover. Every Monday we brought a lot of Marm's cooking from home."

Perhaps the names of some of the principals might be of interest: Charles LeRoy Wheeler, 1880; Gertrude Currier, 1896; Idella K. Farnum, 1900, 1903-1905; Alice M. Walker, 1902-1903; and May A. Miller, 1907-1908. Over the years C. Baldwin, H.B. Dow, and G. Boardman Smith taught in the school. Professor Ephraim Knight of Colby was often engaged as consulting mathematician.

For many years there was a tuition reduction of fifty cents per term for each Wilmot pupil. In the list of expenditures for the town in 1905-1906 there is this item, "Kearsarge School of Practice, fifteen tuitions $34.46." After that year tuition was free for Wilmot boys and girls. During this time there were two terms of school, usually ten weeks each.

By 1912, and perhaps earlier, only one term of ten weeks was held, and this a winter term. At this time the district schools closed early in January and did not reopen until April. Several parents took advantage of this in between period and sent their older children to the Kearsarge School of Practice. Tuition was free, and the course of study included all subjects prescribed by the New Hampshire state program for grades 4 to 9. School was held on the third floor of the building.

For several years the building remained unused. At the annual school meeting in 1921 a committee of five was appointed to investigate and confer with the trustees of the Kearsarge School of Practice to see if an arrangement could be made whereby the town of Wilmot could use the building for studies above the elementary grade level, or benefit from the income of the Youngman-Fisk fund.

The next year an article in the warrant was to hear the report of this committee and to appropriate any money in relation thereafter. It was reported that the trustees agreed to turn over to an elected district committee "such of their yearly income as was deemed advisable, probably not less than $350." Furthermore, the town was to have free use of the building and the trustees were to make necessary alterations and keep the building in repair. Wilmot citizens voted to maintain an approved two-year high school. If at the end of two years the arrangement did not prove workable, it could be terminated by the trustees or the town. The report of the committee was accepted and one thousand dollars was raised for the support of this school. A high school committee of three was elected to serve for one year.

Wilmot's two-year high school opened in the fall of 1922. Miss Ruth G. Chisholm was the principal (and only teacher) for the first two years, and Miss Villa Hall Wight for the third year. Subjects taught were English, history, algebra, Latin, and one-half year each of commercial arithmetic and bookkeeping. The trustees loaned a large number of geographies, histories, English books, and dictionaries in addition to their gift of $350. Classes were held in the first floor corner room toward Bunker Hill.

Fifteen pupils were enrolled the first year, six of these being non-residents. Ten were enrolled the following year with three of these graduating. By the third year of its existence the enrollment had

When School Bells Rang

dropped to four with two of these graduating that May.

Leon R. Sawyer, Lois Sawyer Stanley, and Ruth Stearns Rowe walked seven miles from their homes in North Wilmot each school day they attended.

Graduates in 1924 were Leon R. Sawyer, Wallace S. Thompson, Dean H. Fisher, Ruth A. Johnson, Doris E. Fogg, Helen E. Fogg, and Blanche M. Smith. Ruth M. Stearns and Lois M. Sawyer graduated the following year.

At the school meeting in 1925 it was voted to discontinue the local two-year high school. This was for two reasons: the decrease in the number of pupils and the cost per pupil which was $292.46, the highest of any public high school or academy in the state. The motion was then made and passed that the school board be authorized to confer with the Kearsarge School of Practice Trustees and the probate court in regard to a plan whereby the youth of Wilmot could be permanently benefited. As a result the request was granted. At first the interest of the fund was used for transportation of high school pupils, the money being divided between them. The interest of the fund had to be used for education beyond that which the district provided, therefore, when Wilmot became a part of the Kearsarge Regional School District, a plan of using the money for scholarships was adopted. Any boy or girl beyond the 12th grade may apply for some of this fund.

After the end of the high school the property went through several hands until Richard H. Webb purchased the land and buildings and in 1971 renovated the main building into six apartments, two on each floor.

Epilogue

W ITH THE CLOSING of the Mountain School only two schools remained in the town, one at Wilmot Flat and one at the Center, the two schools having a total enrollment of forty-nine. Gradually the number of elementary school children increased.

A significant change was noted when school opened in September, 1955. For the first time a teacher did not have all eight grades in a building. Instead, the twenty-four pupils in grades 1-4 attended school at the Flat, and twenty-one in grades 5-8 enrolled in the Center school. This arrangement continued until 1958 when the fourth grade was transferred to the Center in order to equalize the teacher load. Even so, there were twenty-eight boys and girls in the first three grades.

At the annual school meeting in March, 1956, questions were raised as to the advisability of maintaining two schools. As a result, a committee was appointed to make a study with the school board regarding the establishment of a central school. The following year this committee stated that to erect a central school building was not feasible for two reasons: (1) No state or federal aid could be obtained for construction of the building, and (2) the borrowing required for such construction under long-term notes would be $48,648, a sum which the town could not afford. At the same time the committee reported "within the next five years we will be faced with inadequate space for the number of pupils in our Elementary Schools."

By 1962-1963 the total pupil enrollment was sixty, and a drastic change was inevitable. Thus the year 1965 marked the first time in 158 years that some of the elementary pupils would not receive their education in Wilmot, for it was this year that grades seven and eight were sent to the New London Central School as tuition pupils.

The last school meeting of the town was held on March 11, 1967. Elected officers were to serve only until July first of that year because on that date Wilmot was to become a member of the Kearsarge Regional School District. This decision had been reached at a special meeting on February 19, 1959, when it was voted to petition the State Board of Education to become a member of a regional school district which would include a group of neighboring towns. The vote was thirty-five in favor and thirteen opposed. Final approval on May 2, 1966, resulted in New London, Springfield, Bradford, Newbury, Sutton, Warner, and Wilmot becoming members of the Kearsarge Regional School District.

Perhaps this important change can best be summed up in words of the School Board for 1966:

So change has come and continues, but although there is a certain nostalgic sadness in the closing of what might be called an era, there is pride that Wilmot has never hesitated when confronted by a decision affecting the welfare and potential future of its children.

Alterations and additions to the New London central school building were necessary to accommodate the expected increase of pupils, therefore grades one through six still attended the Wilmot schools until 1970. That fall parents of first and second graders were given a choice of sending their children to the Flat School or to New London. As a result, seven enrolled in the Wilmot school and eighteen in New London.

There were other district changes evident in September, 1970. Grades 1-5 were held in the New London Central School and grades 6-8 in the New London Middle School. A school bus transported the Wilmot pupils to the New London schools five or six miles away. A new high school in Sutton, known as the Kearsarge Regional High School, opened that same year.

What became of Wilmot's two schoolhouses? At the annual district meeting in March, 1972, it was voted to authorize the school board to sell and convey the Wilmot Center Schoolhouse and land for

                                            When School Bells Rang

the sum of one dollar to the Town of Wilmot. This was with the understanding that if the land was not used for library or other town purposes it would revert to the school district. As stated elsewhere, the building now houses the public library. Two years later the school district voted to sell the Wilmot Flat Schoolhouse for one dollar to the Town of Wilmot for town purposes. The building has since been remodeled so that it contains a historical room, a meeting room, and rooms for town offices.

Town taxpayers are aware of the steady increase in the cost of educating Wilmot's pupils. By the Articles of Agreement of the District the expenses are to be apportioned 75% upon the number of pupils residing in the member community, and 25% on the equalized valuation of each town. With a total enrollment of 102 in 1970, Wilmot paid the school district $80,208.02. In 1975 the enrollment was 132 and the cost of education was $190,482.90.

No longer do the children of Wilmot enter a one-room schoolhouse at the sound of the teacher's hand bell. No sound of children's voices will be heard in the school yard where once the children played. When school is in session the town is empty of school-age children for six or seven hours each day. Secondary pupils leave on busses for the high school in Sutton, a distance of approximately ten miles. Because of the distance their day is a longer one, some must leave home as early as seven o'clock and will not return until four.

The old order has changed and yielded place to new, but Wilmot has not, and will not, shirk its responsibility of providing education for its children.

BIBLIOGRAPHY

Town Histories
      Andover, N.H., (1751-1966), by John R. Eastman
      New London, N.H., by Myra B. Lord, 1899
      Sutton, N.H.
      Wilmot, N.H., by Casper L. LeVarn, 1957
Annual Town reports of Wilmot, 1878-1975
Annual School Reports of Wilmot, 1878-1967
Annual Reports Upon the Common Schools of N.H.
N.H. State Board of Education Reports, 1933-1935
New Hampshire Revised Statutes, 2 vol., 1842-1867
Written Records of Wilmot School Districts
      District 1, 1860-1880
      District 2, 1815-1845
      District 8, 1841-1885
      District 10, 1843-1849
      District 11, 1843-1870
Annual Reports of Kearsarge Regional School District, 1968-1976
Circulars of Kearsarge School of Practice, 1876, 1884, 1896, 1900, 1902-1904, 1911-1913,
      1914-1915
The Government of New Hampshire (revised edition 1952), Leonard S. Morrison
New Hampshire Laws
Merrimack County Registry of Deeds
Notes of Reminiscences
      Sarah Teel, 1914
      Joshua Holland, 1916
      Seldon Tewksbury
Letters
      Elisha K. Morrill to George B. Tewksbury, 1906
      Asenath Upton Stevens to Wilmot History Comm. 1915
School registers of Wilmot

When School Bells Rang

When School Bells Rang

When School Bells Rang